Defoe Abbott Marx Hardy Melville Montaigne Machiavelli Haggard Chesterton Cooper Emerson Joyce Austen Hugo Eliot Grimm

Stoker Carroll Christie Maupassant Molière Byron Schiller

Wilde Garnett Einstein Fitzgerald Engels Hawthorne Smith Kafka Hall

Goethe Cotton Dostoyevsky Kipling Doyle Willis

Baum Henry Nietzsche Balzac

Leslie Dumas Flaubert Turgenev Vatsyayana Crane

Stockton Verne Vinci

Burroughs Whitman Gogol Busch

Curtis Tocqueville

Homer Widger Tolstoy Twain Scott Plato Harte

Darwin Thoreau

Potter Freud Zola Lawrence Dickens Burton Hesse

Kant Jowett Stevenson

Andersen Cervantes Voltaire

London Descartes Wells Cooke

Poe Aristotle

Hale James Hastings Irving

Bunner Shakespeare

Richter Chambers da Shaw Benedict Alcott

Doré Dante Chekhov Wodehouse Pushkin

Swift Newton

tredition

tredition was established in 2006 by Sandra Latusseck and Soenke Schulz. Based in Hamburg, Germany, tredition offers publishing solutions to authors and publishing houses, combined with world-wide distribution of printed and digital book content. tredition is uniquely positioned to enable authors and publishing houses to create books on their own terms and without conventional manu-facturing risks.

For more information please visit: www.tredition.com

TREDITION CLASSICS

This book is part of the TREDITION CLASSICS series. The creators of this series are united by passion for literature and driven by the intention of making all public domain books available in printed format again - worldwide. Most TREDITION CLASSICS titles have been out of print and off the bookstore shelves for decades. At tredition we believe that a great book never goes out of style and that its value is eternal. Several mostly non-profit literature projects provide content to tredition. To support their good work, tredition donates a portion of the proceeds from each sold copy. As a reader of a TREDITION CLASSICS book, you support our mission to save many of the amazing works of world literature from oblivion. See all available books at www.tredition.com.

 Project Gutenberg

The content for this book has been graciously provided by Project Gutenberg. Project Gutenberg is a non-profit organization founded by Michael Hart in 1971 at the University of Illinois. The mission of Project Gutenberg is simple: To encourage the creation and distribution of eBooks. Project Gutenberg is the first and largest collection of public domain eBooks.

Indians of the Yosemite Valley and Vicinity Their History, Customs and Traditions

Galen Clark

Imprint

This book is part of TREDITION CLASSICS

Author: Galen Clark
Cover design: Buchgut, Berlin – Germany

Publisher: tredition GmbH, Hamburg - Germany
ISBN: 978-3-8424-8181-7

www.tredition.com
www.tredition.de

Photograph by Tabor.
Galen Clark

Frontispiece

Yours Sincerely
Galen Clark
Yosemite Calif.

Author's Inscription

Contents

List of Illustrations

Introduction and Sketch of the Author

Galen Clark, the author of this little volume, is one of the notable characters of California, and the one best fitted to record the customs and traditions of the Yosemite Indians, but it was only after much persuasion that his friends succeeded in inducing him to write the history of these interesting people, with whom he has been in close communication for half a century.

The Indians of the Yosemite are fast passing away. Only a handful now remain of the powerful tribes that once gathered in the Valley and considered it an absolute stronghold against their white enemies. Even in their diminished numbers and their comparatively civilized condition, they are still a source of great interest to all visitors, and it has been suggested many times that their history, customs and legends should be put in permanent and convenient form, before they are entirely lost.

Many tales and histories of the California Indians have been written by soldiers and pioneers, but Mr. Clark has told the story of these people from their own standpoint, and with a sympathetic understanding of their character. This fresh point of view gives double interest to his narrative.

Galen Clark comes of a notable family; his English ancestors came to the State of Massachusetts in the seventeenth century, but he is a native of the Town of Dublin, Cheshire County, New Hampshire, born on the 28th day of March, 1814, and is consequently nearly ninety years of age, but still alert and active in mind and body.

He attended school in his early youth during the winter months, and worked on a farm during the summer, leading nearly the same life which was followed by so many others who afterwards became famous in our country's history.

Later in life he learned chair-making and painting, an occupation which he followed for some years, when he removed to Philadelphia and subsequently to New York City.

Whilst residing in New York, in 1853, he resolved, after mature reflection, to visit the new Eldorado. His attention was first attracted to this State by visiting the celebrated Crystal Palace in New

York, where was then on exhibition quantities of gold dust which had been sent or brought East by successful miners.

Mr. Clark left New York for California in October, 1853, coming via the Isthmus of Panama, and in due time reached his destination. In 1854 he went to Mariposa County, attracted thither by the wonderful accounts of the gold discoveries, and the marvelous stories he had heard of the grandeur and beauty of the Yosemite Valley and the surrounding mountains.

Upon his first arrival in Mariposa, he engaged in mining, and was also employed to assist in surveying Government land on the west side of the San Joaquin Valley, and canals for mining purposes, some of which passed through the celebrated "Mariposa Grant," the subject of prolonged and bitter litigation, both in this country and in Europe. He probably knows more about the actual facts concerning the Mariposa Grant than any one now living, and it is to be hoped that some day he may overcome his natural repugnance to notoriety, and give to the public the benefit of his knowledge.

In the year 1855 Mr. Clark made his first trip into the Yosemite Valley with a party made up in Mariposa and Bear Valley.

Returning to Mariposa, he resumed his old occupation of surveying and mining, and, whilst so engaged, by reason of exposure, had a serious attack of lung trouble, resulting in severe hemorrhages which threatened to end his life.

He then removed, in April, 1857, to the South Fork of the Merced River, and built a log cabin in one of the most beautiful of our mountain valleys, on the spot where Wawona now stands. He soon recovered his health entirely, and, though constantly exposed to the winter storms and snows, has never had a recurrence of his malady.

Wawona is twenty-six miles from Yosemite, and at that time became known as Clark's Station, being on the trail leading from Mariposa to the Valley, and a noted stopping place for travelers. This trail, as well as one from Coulterville, was completed to the Valley in 1857, and the trip to Yosemite then involved a stage ride of ninety-two miles, and a journey of sixty miles more on horseback. In 1874 and 1875 the three present stage roads were constructed through to the Valley.

All travelers by the Raymond route will remember Wawona and the surroundings; the peaceful valley, the swift-flowing Merced, and the surrounding peaks and mountains, almost equaling in grandeur the famous Yosemite itself.

In the early days this locality was annually visited by several bands of Indians from the Chowchilla and Fresno rivers. The Indian name for the place was Pal-lah´-chun. Whilst residing there Mr. Clark was in constant contact with these visiting tribes; he obtained their confidence, and retains it to this day.

Whilst on a hunting trip, in the summer of 1857, Mr. Clark discovered and made known to the public the famous Big Tree Grove, now known all over the world as the "Mariposa Grove of Big Trees," belonging to the State of California. On this expedition he did not follow the route now traveled, but came upon the grove at the upper end, near the place where the road to Wawona Point now branches off from the main drive. The spot where he caught his first view of the Big Trees has been appropriately marked, and can be seen from the stage road.

So impressed was Mr. Clark with the importance of his discovery, that he opened up a good horse trail from Wawona to the Trees, and shortly afterwards built a log cabin in the grove, for the comfort and convenience of visitors in bad or stormy weather. This cabin became known as "Galen's Hospice."

In the year 1864 the Congress of the United States passed an Act, which was approved in June of the same year, granting to the State of California the "Yosemite Valley" and the "Mariposa Grove of Big Trees." This grant was made upon certain conditions, which were complied with by the State, and a Commission was appointed by Governor Low to manage and govern the Valley and the Big Tree Grove. Galen Clark was, of course, selected as one of the commissioners. He was subsequently appointed Guardian of the Valley, and under his administration many needed improvements were made and others suggested. Bridges were built, roads constructed on the floor of the Valley, and trails laid out and finished to various points of interest overlooking the Valley itself. In a word, the Guardian did everything possible with the limited means at his disposal.

After serving twenty-four years, Mr. Clark voluntarily retired from the position of Guardian, carrying with him the respect and admiration of every member of the Commission, of all the residents of the Valley, and of every visitor who enjoyed the pleasure of his personal acquaintance.

As showing the opinion of those with whom Mr. Clark was intimately and officially associated for so long a time, the following resolutions passed by the Board of Commissioners upon his voluntary retirement from the office of Guardian, are herein given:

Whereas, Galen Clark has for a long number of years been closely identified with Yosemite Valley, and has for a considerable portion of that time been its Guardian; and

Whereas, he has now, by his own choice and will, relinquished the trust confided in him and retired into private life; and

Whereas, his faithful and eminent services as Guardian, his constant efforts to preserve, protect and enhance the beauties of Yosemite; his dignified, kindly and courteous demeanor to all who have come to see and enjoy its wonders, and his upright and noble life, deserve from us a fitting recognition and memorial; Now, Therefore, be it

Resolved, That the cordial assurance of the appreciation by this Commission of the efforts and labors of Galen Clark, as Guardian of Yosemite, in its behalf, be tendered and expressed to him.

That we recognize in him a faithful, efficient and worthy citizen and officer of this Commission and of the State; that he will be followed into his retirement by the sincerest and best wishes of this Commission, individually and as a body, for continued long life and constant happiness.

The subject of this sketch is one of the most modest of men; but perfectly self-reliant, and always actively engaged in some useful work. He has resided in the Valley for more than twenty summers, and has also been a resident during many winters, and his descriptions of the Valley, when wrapped in snow and ice, are intensely interesting. Though always ready to give information, he is naturally reticent, and never forces his stories or reminiscences upon visitors; indeed it requires some persuasion to hear him talk about himself at all.

For some years Mr. Clark was postmaster of Yosemite; and he has made many trips on foot, both in winter and summer, in and out of the Valley.

In September, 1903, this writer made a trip through the high Sierras from Yosemite, and, upon reaching the top of the Valley Mr. Clark was met coming down the trail, having in charge a party of his friends, amongst whom was a lady with her two small children. This was at a point 2700 feet above the floor of the Valley, which is itself 4000 feet above the level of the sea.

Needless to say, he is perfectly familiar with all the mountain trails, and, notwithstanding his great age, he easily makes long trips on foot and horseback which would fatigue a much younger man. Mr. Clark is thoroughly familiar with the flora, fauna and geology of the Valley and its surroundings. His knowledge of botany is particularly accurate, a knowledge gleaned partly from books, but mainly from close personal observation, the best possible teacher.

His long residence in Yosemite has made him familiar with every spot, his love for the Valley is deep and strong, and when he departs this life his remains will rest close to the Yosemite Falls, in the little grave yard where other pioneers are buried.

With his own hands he has dug his grave, and quarried his own tombstone from one of the massive blocks of granite found in the immediate neighborhood. His monument now rests in his grave, and when it is removed to receive his remains, will be used to mark his last resting place. His grave is surrounded by a neat fence, and trees, shrubs and vines, which he has himself planted, grow around in great profusion. In each corner of the lot is a young *Sequoia*.

May it be many years before he is called to occupy his last earthly tenement.

W.W. FOOTE.

San Francisco, February, 1904.

INDIANS OF THE YOSEMITE

Chapter One.

EARLY HISTORY.

During the past few years a rapidly growing interest in the native Indians has been manifested by a large majority of visitors to the Yosemite Valley. They have evinced a great desire to see them in their rudely constructed summer camps, and to purchase some articles of their artistic basket and bead work, to take away as highly prized souvenirs.

They are also anxious to learn something of their former modes of life, habits and domestic industries, before their original tribal relations were ruthlessly broken up by the sudden advent of the white population of gold miners and others in 1850, and the subsequent war, in which the Indians were defeated, and, as a result, nearly exterminated.

ORIGIN OF THE YOSEMITE INDIANS.

According to statements made by Teneiya *(Ten-eye´-ya)* [see footnote] chief of the Yosemites, to Dr. L.H. Bunnell, and published by him in his book on the "Discovery of the Yosemite", the original Indian name of the Valley was Ah-wah´-nee, which has been translated as "deep grassy valley", and the Indians living there were called Ah-wah-nee´-chees, which signified "dwellers in Ah-wah´-nee."

Footnote: The Indian names are usually pronounced exactly as spelled, with each syllable distinctly sounded, and the principal accent on the penult, as in Ah-wah´-nee, or the antepenult, as in Yo-sem´-i-te. Where doubt might exist, the accent will be indicated, or the pronunciation given in parenthesis.

Transcriber's note: The remaining footnotes in the original text are, in the present edition, moved into the line of text and are marked by square brackets, thus: Ah-wah´-nee [Yosemite Valley].

Many years ago, the old chief said, the Ah-wah-nee´-chees had been a large and powerful tribe, but by reason of wars and a fatal black sickness, nearly all had been destroyed, and the survivors of the band fled from the Valley and joined other tribes.

YOSEMITE FALLS (CHO´-LACK), 2,634 Feet.

Near the foot of these falls was located the village of Ah-wah´-nee, the Indian capital and residence of Chief Teneiya. There were eight other villages in the Valley.

For years afterwards this locality was uninhabited, but finally Teneiya, who claimed to be descended from an Ah-wah-nee´-chee chief, left the Mo´nos, where he had born and brought up, and, gathering of his father's old tribe around him, visited the Valley and claimed it as the birthright of his people. He then became the founder of a new tribe or band, which received the name "Yo-sem´-i-te." This word signifies a full-grown grizzly bear, and Teneiya said that the name had been given to his band because they occupied the mountains and valley which were the favorite resort of the grizzly bears, and his people were expert in killing them; that his tribe had adopted the name because those who had bestowed it were afraid of the grizzlies, and also feared his band.

The Yosemites were perhaps the most warlike of any of the tribes in this part of the Sierra Nevada Mountains, who were, as a rule, a peaceful people, dividing the territory among them, and indulging in few controversies. In fact, these Indians in general were less belligerent and warlike than any others on the Pacific Coast. When difficulties arose, they were usually settled peacefully by arbitration, in a grand council of the chiefs and head men of the tribes involved, without resorting to open hostilities.

OTHER TRIBES.

Other bands of Indians in the vicinity of the Yosemite Valley were the Po-ho-nee´-chees who lived near the headwaters of the Po-ho´-no or Bridal Veil Creek in summer, and on the South Fork of the Merced´ River in winter, about twelve miles below Wawo´na; the Po-to-en´-cies, who lived on the Merced River; Wil-tuc-um´-nees, Tuol´-unme River; Noot´-choos and Chow-chil´-las, Chowchilla Valley; Ho-na´-ches and Me´-woos, Fresno River and vicinity; and Chook-chan´-ces, San Joaquin River and vicinity.

These tribes, including the Yosemites, were all somewhat affiliated by common ancestry or by intermarriage, and were similar in their general characteristics and customs. They were all called by the early California settlers, "Digger Indians," as a term of derision, on account of their not being good fighters, and from their practice of digging the tuberous roots of certain plants, for food.

INDIAN WAR OF 1851.

Dr. Bunnell, in his book already referred to, has given the soldiers' and white men's account of the cause of the Indian war of 1851, but a statement of the grievances on the part of the Indians, which caused the uniting of all the different tribes in the mining region adjacent to Yosemite, in an attempt to drive the white invaders from their country, has never been published, and a brief account of these grievances may be interesting.

AGGRESSIONS BY THE WHITE SETTLERS.

The first parties of prospecting miners were welcomed by the Indians with their usual friendliness and hospitality toward strangers—a universal characteristic of these tribes,—and the mining for gold was watched with great interest. They soon learned the value of the gold dust, and some of them engaged in mining, and exchanged their gold at the trading stations for blankets and fancy trinkets, at an enormous profit to the traders, and peace and good feeling prevailed for a short time.

EARLY HISTORY.

The report of the rich gold "diggin's" on the waters of the Tuolumne, Merced, Mariposa, Chowchilla, and Fresno Rivers, soon spread, and miners by thousands came and took possession of the whole country, paying no regard to the natural rights or wishes of the Indians.

Some of the Indian chiefs made the proposition that if the miners would give them some of the gold which they found in their part of the country, they might stay and work. This offer was not listened to by the miners, and a large majority of the white invaders treated the natives as though they had no rights whatever to be respected.

In some instances, where Indians had found and were working good mining claims, they were forcibly driven away by white miners, who took possession of their claims and worked them.

Moreover, the Indians saw that their main sources of food supply were being rapidly destroyed. The oak trees, which produced the acorns—one of their staple articles of food,—were being cut down and burned by miners and others in clearing up land for cultivation, and the deer and other food game were being rapidly killed off or driven from the locality.

AN INDIAN DANCER.

Chow-chil-la Indian in full war-dance costume.

In the "early days," before California was admitted as a free State into the Union, it was reported, and was probably true, that some of the immigrants from the slave-holding States took Indians and made slaves of them in working their mining claims. It was no uncommon event for the sanctity of their homes and families to be invaded by some of the "baser sort," and young women taken, willing or not, for servants and wives.

RETALIATION.

In retaliation, and as some compensation for these many grievous outrages upon their natural inalienable rights of domain and property, and their native customs, the Indians stole horses and mules from the white settlers, and killed them for food for their families, who, in many instances, were in a condition of starvation.

Finally the chiefs and leading men of all the tribes involved met in a grand council, and resolved to combine their warrior forces in one great effort to drive all their white enemies from the country, before they became more numerous and formidable.

BEGINNING OF HOSTILITIES.

To prepare for this struggle for existence, they made raids upon some of the principal trading posts in the mining sections, killed those in charge, took all the blankets, clothing and provisions they could carry away, and fled to the mountains, where they were soon pursued by the soldiers and volunteer citizens, and a spirited battle was fought without any decisive advantage to either side.

The breaking out of actual hostilities created great excitement among the whites, and an urgent call was made upon the Governor of the State for a military force to meet the emergency, and protect the settlers—a force strong enough to thoroughly subdue the Indians, and remove all of them to reservations to be selected by the United States Indian Commissioners for that purpose.

Meantime the Governor and the Commissioners, who had then arrived, were receiving numerous communications, many of them from persons in high official positions, earnestly urging a more humane and just policy, averring that the Indians had real cause for complaint, that they had been "more sinned against than sinning" since the settling of California by the whites, and that they were justly entitled to protection by the Government and compensation for the spoliations and grievances they had suffered.

These protests doubtless had some influence in delaying hostile measures, and in the inauguration of efforts to induce the Indians to come in and treat with the Commissioners, envoys being sent out to assure them of fair treatment and personal safety. Many of the Indians accepted these offers, and, as the different tribes surrendered, they were taken to the two reservations which the Commissioners had established for them on the Fresno River, the principal one being a few miles above the place where the town of Madera is now located.

As before stated, these Indians were not a warlike people. Their only weapons were their bows and arrows, and these they soon found nearly useless in defending themselves at long range against soldiers armed with rifles. Moreover, their stock of provisions was so limited that they either had to surrender or starve.

DISCOVERY OF YOSEMITE VALLEY.

The Yosemites and one or two other bands of Indians had refused to surrender, and had retreated to their mountain strongholds, where they proposed to make a last determined resistance. Active preparations were accordingly made by the State authorities to follow them, and either capture or exterminate all the tribes involved. For this purpose a body of State volunteers, known as the Mariposa Battalion, was organized, under the command of Major James D. Savage, to pursue these tribes into the mountains; and, after many long marches and some fighting, the Indians were all defeated, captured, and, with their women and children, put upon the reservations under strong military guard.

It was during this campaign that Major Savage and his men discovered the Yosemite Valley, about the 21st of March, 1851, while in pursuit of the Yosemites, under old Chief Teneiya, for whom Lake Teneiya and Teneiya Canyon have appropriately been named.

THREE BROTHERS (WAW-HAW´-KEE), 3,900 Feet.

Named by the soldiers who discovered the Valley, to commemorate the capture of three sons of Teneiya near this place. The Indian name means "Falling Rocks."

Chapter Two.

EFFECTS OF THE WAR.

The Yosemites and all of the other tribes named in the previous chapter were put upon the Fresno reservation. Major Savage, who had been the leading figure in the war against the Indians, was perhaps their best friend while in captivity, and finally lost his life in a personal quarrel, while resenting a wrong which had been committed against them.

The tribes from south of the San Joaquin River, who were also conquered in 1851, were put upon the Kings River and Tejon (*Tay-hone´*) reservations.

LIFE ON THE RESERVATIONS.

Ample food supplies, blankets, clothing and cheap fancy articles were furnished by the Government for the subsistence, comfort and pleasure of the Indians on the reservations, and for a short time they seemed to be contented, and to enjoy the novelty of their new mode of life. The young, able-bodied men were put to work assisting in clearing, fencing and cultivating fields for hay and vegetables, and thus they were partially self-supporting. A large portion of them, however, soon began to tire of the restraints imposed, and longed for their former condition of freedom, and many of them sickened and died.

Old Teneiya, chief of the "Grizzlies," was particularly affected by the change in his surroundings, and by the humiliation of defeat. He suffered keenly from the hot weather of the plains, after his free life in the mountains, and begged to be allowed to return to his old home, promising not to disturb the white settlers in any way, a pledge which he did not break.

DEATH OF TENEIYA.

Teneiya was finally allowed to depart, with his family, after having been on the reservation only a few months, and some of his old followers afterwards stole away and joined him. With this remnant of his band he returned to the Yosemite, but not long afterwards they were set upon by the Monos, a tribe from the eastern side of the Sierras, with whom they had quarreled, and the old chief and many of his warriors were killed. It was perhaps fitting that he should meet his death in the valley which he loved, and which he had so long defended against his enemies.

RESTORED TO LIBERTY.

In 1855, after four years of confinement on the reservations, an agreement was made with the Indian Commissioners, by the head men of the tribes, that if their people were again allowed their freedom, they would forever remain in peace with the white settlers, and try and support themselves free of expense to the Government. They were soon permitted to leave, and have ever since faithfully kept their promise.

Most of them went back to the vicinity of their old homes, and made temporary settlements on unoccupied Government land, as many of their old village sites were now in possession of white settlers. As there was a very large crop of acorns that season, they gathered an abundant supply for winter use, and, with what was given to them in the way of food and clothing by some of the white settlers, they managed to get through the winter fairly well.

CAPTAIN PAUL.

One of the characters of the Valley. Supposed to be 105 years old, and a survivor of Teneiya's band.

HARDSHIP AND SUFFERING.

Their four years' residence on the reservations, however, had been more of a school in the vices of the whites than one of a higher education. They became demoralized socially, addicted to many bad habits, and left the reservations in worse condition than when they were taken there. Their old tribal relations and customs were nearly broken up, though they still had their head men to whom they looked for counsel in all important matters.

As the country became more settled, much of their main food supply, the acorns, was consumed by the domestic animals of the ranchers, and their mode of living became more precarious and transitory, and many of them were, at times, in a condition near to starvation. In these straitened and desperate circumstances, many of their young women were used as commercial property, and peddled out to the mining camps and gambling saloons for money to buy food, clothing or whisky, this latter article being obtained through the aid of some white person, in violation of law.

Their miserable, squalid condition of living opened the way for diseases of a malignant character, which their medicine men could not cure, and their numbers were rapidly reduced by death.

At the present time there are not in existence a half-dozen of the old Yosemites who were living, even as children, when the Valley was first discovered in 1851; and many of the other tribes have been correspondingly reduced.>

YOSEMITE MOTHER AND PAPOOSE.

The baby basket is carried on the back, like all burdens, and supported by a band across the forehead.

Chapter Three.

CUSTOMS AND CHARACTERISTICS.

As stated in a previous chapter, all of the Indian tribes occupying the region in the vicinity of the Yosemite Valley were more or less affiliated by blood and intermarriage and resembled each other in their customs, characteristics and religious beliefs. What is said, therefore, on these subjects in the following pages, will be understood to apply generally to all of the tribes which have been mentioned as inhabiting this region, although, of course, minor differences did exist, principally due to environment. As in the case of all primitive peoples, their mode of life, food supply, etc., were largely determined by natural conditions, and the tribes living in the warm foot-hills differed somewhat in these respects from those dwelling higher in the mountains.

DIVISION OF TERRITORY.

In their original tribal settlements, at the time the first pioneer whites came among them, the Indians had well defined or understood boundary lines, between the territories claimed by each tribe for their exclusive use in hunting game and gathering means of support; and any trespassing on the domain of others was likely to cause trouble. This arrangement, however, did not apply to the higher ranges of the Sierras, which were considered common hunting ground.

COMMERCE AMONG THE TRIBES.

As there was a difference in the natural products and resources of different sections of the country, there was a system of reciprocal trade in the exchange of the different desirable commodities. Sometimes commerce between tribes extended for a long distance, as, for instance, the Indians on the western side of the Sierra Nevada Mountains were entirely dependent upon the Pai-utes *(Pye-yutes´)* on the eastern side for the obsidian, a kind of volcanic glass, from which they made the points for their most deadly arrows, used in hunting large game or when in mortal combat with their enemies. They were also dependent upon the Pai-utes for their supply of salt for domestic use, which came in solid blocks as quarried from salt mines, said to be two days' travel on foot from Mono Lake.

From the Indians at or near the Catholic Missions to the South, on the Pacific Coast, they got their hunting knives of iron or steel, and sea shells of various kinds, for personal or dress ornaments, and also to be used as money. From the same source they obtained beads of various forms, sizes and colors, cheap jewelry and other fancy articles, a few blankets, and pieces of red bunting, strips of which the chiefs and head men wore around their heads as badges, indicating their official positions.

COMMUNICATION.

They had a very efficient system of quickly spreading important news by relays of special couriers, who took the news to the first stations or tribes in different directions, where others took the verbal dispatches and ran to the next station, and so on, so that all tribes within an area of a hundred miles would get the good or bad tidings within a few hours. In this manner important communication was kept up between the different tribes. They also had well organized signal systems, by fires in the night and smoke by day, on high points of observation—variations in the lights (either steady, bright or flashing) indicating somewhat the character of the tidings thus given.

DWELLINGS.

Their winter huts, or *o´-chums*, as they termed them, were invariably of a conical form, made with small poles, and covered with the bark of the incense cedar (*Libocedrus decurrens*). A few poles ten or twelve feet long were set in the ground around an area of about twelve feet in diameter, with their tops inclined together. The outside was then closely covered with long strips of the cedar bark, making it perfectly water-tight. An opening was left on the south side for an entrance, which could be readily closed with a portable door. An opening was also left at the top for the escape of the smoke, a fire being kindled in the center inside.

INDIAN O´-CHUM.

This style of house, made of cedar poles covered with bark, is more easily heated than any other form of dwelling known.

One of these huts would hold a family of a half-dozen persons, with all their household property, dogs included; and there is no other form of a single-room dwelling that can be kept warm and comfortable in cold weather with so little fire, as this Indian *o´-chum.*

Their under-bedding usually consisted of the skins of bears, deer, antelope or elk, and the top covering was a blanket or robe made of the skins of small fur-bearing animals, such as rabbits, hares, wild-cats and foxes. The skins were cut in narrow strips, which were loosely twisted so as to bring the fur entirely around on the outside, and then woven into a warp of strong twine made of the fine, tough, fibrous bark of a variety of milkweed (*Asclepias speciosa*). These fur robes were very warm, and were also used as wraps when traveling in cold weather.

During the warm summer season they generally lived outside in brush arbors, and used their *o´-chums* as storage places.

YOSEMITE MAIDEN IN NATIVE DRESS.

This buckskin costume has now been replaced by the unpicturesque calico of civilization.

CLOTHING.

Their clothing was very simple and scant, before being initiated into the use of a more ample and complete style of covering while living at the reservations. The ordinary full complement of dress for a man (*Nung´-ah*) was simply a breech-clout, or short hip-skirt made of skins; that for a woman (*O´-hoh*) was a skirt reaching from the waist to the knees, made of dressed deerskin finished at the bottom with a slit fringe, and sometimes decorated with various fancy ornaments. Both men and women frequently wore moccasins made of dressed deer or elk skin. Young children generally went entirely nude.

CHARACTERISTICS.

The Indians of the various tribes in this part of the Sierras vary somewhat in physical characteristics, but in general are of medium height, strong, lean and agile, and the men are usually fine specimens of manhood. They are rather light in color, but frequently rub their bodies with some kind of oil, which gives the flesh a much redder and more glossy appearance. The hair is black and straight, and the eyes are black and deep set. The beard is sparse, and in former times was not allowed to grow at all, each hair being pulled out with a rude kind of tweezers. They are naturally of a gentle and friendly disposition, but their experience with the white race has made them distant and uncommunicative to strangers.

Most of the older Indians still cling to their old customs and manner of living, and are very slow to learn or talk our language, but the younger ones are striving to live like the white people, and seem proud to adopt our style of dress and manner of cooking. They all speak our language plainly, and some few of them attend the public schools when living near by, and acquire very readily the common rudiments of an education.

Their style of architecture is in a state of transition, like themselves. Their old *o´-chum* form of dwelling is now very seldom seen—a rude building of more roomy and modern design having taken its place.

All the able-bodied men are ready and willing to work at any kind of common labor, when they have an opportunity, and have learned to want nearly the same amount of pay as a white man for the same work.

As a rule, they are trustworthy, and when confidence is placed in their honesty it is very rarely betrayed. During nearly the past fifty years, a great many thousands of people have visited the Yosemite Valley with their own camping outfits, and, during the day, and often all night, are absent on distant trips of observation, with no one left in charge of camp, yet there has never to my knowledge been an instance of anything being stolen or molested by Indians. There are, however, some dishonest Indians, who will steal from their own people, and some times, when a long distance from their own camp, they may steal from the whites. A few, if they can get whisky, through the aid of some white person, will become drunk and fight among themselves, and occasionally one of them may be killed; but, as a rule, they are peaceful and orderly, and hold sacred the promise made to the Indian Commissioners by the old tribal chiefs, when released from confinement on the reservations, that they would forever keep the peace, and never again make war against the white people.

Chapter Four.

SOURCES OF FOOD SUPPLY.

The food supply of the Sierra Indians was extensive and abundant, consisting of the flesh of deer, antelope, elk and mustang horses, together with fish, water-fowls, birds, acorns, berries, pine nuts, esculent herbage and the tuberous roots of certain plants, all of which were easily obtained, even with their simple and limited means of securing them. Mushrooms, fungi, grasshoppers, worms and the larvae of ants and other insects, were also eaten, and some of these articles were considered great delicacies.

HUNTING.

Their main effective weapons for hunting large game were their bows and obsidian-pointed arrows. Their manner of hunting was either by the stealthy still hunt, or a general turn-out, surrounding a large area of favorable country and driving to a common center, where at close range the hunters could sometimes make an extensive slaughter.

Drawing by Jorgensen.

A YOSEMITE HUNTER.

He wears a false deer's head, to deceive the game.

When on the still hunt for deer in the brushy, sparsely timbered foothills of the Sierra Range of mountains, or higher up in the extensive forests, some of the hunters wore for a headgear a false deer's head, by which deceptive device they were enabled to get to a closer and more effective range with their bows and arrows. This head-dress was made of the whole skin of a doe's head, with a part of the neck, the head part stuffed with light material, the eyeholes filled in with the green feathered scalp of a duck's head, and the top furnished with light wooden horns, the branching stems of the manzanita (*Arctostaphylos*) being generally used for this purpose. The neck part was made to fit on the hunter's head and fasten with strings tied under the chin. This unique style of headgear was used by some Indian hunters for many years after they had guns to hunt with.

The high ranges of the mountains, as already stated, were considered common hunting ground by the different tribes. The deer, many of them, were in some degree migratory in their habits, being driven from the higher ranges to the foothills by the deep winter snows, and in the spring following close to the melting, receding snow, back again to their favorite summer haunts.

Drawing by Jorgensen

INDIAN SWEAT HOUSE.

Used by the Yosemite hunters before starting after game.

Late in the summer, or early in the fall, just before holding some of their grand social or sacred festivals, the Indian hunters would make preparation for a big hunt in the mountains, to get a good supply of venison for the feast. One of the first absolute prerequisites was to go through a thorough course of sweating and personal cleansing. This was done by resorting to their sweat houses, which were similar in construction to the *o´-chums*, except that the top was rounded and the whole structure was covered thickly with mud and earth to exclude the air. These houses were heated with hot stones and coals of fire, and the hunters would then crawl into them and remain until in a profuse perspiration, when they would come out and plunge into cold water for a wash-off. This was repeated until they thought themselves sufficiently free from all bodily odor so that the deer could not detect their approach by scent, and flee for safety.

After this purification they kept themselves strictly as celibates until the hunt was over, though their women went along to help carry the outfit, keep camp, cook, search for berries and pine nuts, and assist in bringing to camp and taking care of the deer as killed, and in "packing" the meat out to the place of rendezvous appointed for the grand ceremonies and feast.

Their usual manner of cooking fresh meat was by broiling on hot coals, or roasting before the fire or in the embers. Sometimes, however, they made a cavity in the ground, in which they built a fire, which was afterwards cleared away and the cavity lined with very hot stones, on which they placed the meat wrapped in green herbage, and covered it with other hot rocks and earth, to remain until suitably cooked.

When they had a surplus of fresh meat they cut it in strips and hung it in the sun-shine to dry. The dried meat was generally cooked by roasting in hot embers, and then beaten to soften it before being eaten.

A young hunter never ate any of the first deer he killed, as he believed that if he did so he would never succeed in killing another.

FISHING.

They had various methods of catching fish — with hook and line, with a spear, by weir-traps in the stream, and by saturating the water with the juice of the soap-root plant (*Chlorogalum pomeridi-*

anum). Before they could obtain fishhooks of modern make, they made them of bone. Their lines were made of the tough, fibrous, silken bark of the variety of milkweed or silkweed, already mentioned. Their spears were small poles pointed with a single tine of bone, which was so arranged that it became detached by the struggles of the fish, and was then held by a string fastened near its center, which turned it crosswise of the wound and made it act as an effective barb.

Their weir-traps were put in the rapids, and constructed by building wing dams diagonally down to the middle of the stream until the two ends came near together, and in this narrow outlet was placed a sort of wicker basket trap, made of long willow sprouts loosely woven together and closed at the pointed lower end, which was elevated above the surface of the water below the dam. The fish, in going down stream, ran into this trap, and soon found themselves at the lower end and out of the water.

The soap-root was used at a low stage of water, late in summer. They dug several bushels of the bulbous roots and went to a suitable place on the bank, where the roots were pounded into a pulp, and mixed with soil and water. This mixture, by the handful, was then rubbed on rocks out in the stream, which roiled the water and also made it somewhat foamy. The fish were soon affected by it, became stupid with a sort of strangulation, and rose to the surface, where they were easily captured by the Indians with their scoop baskets. In a stream the size of the South Fork of the Merced River at Wawona, by this one operation every fish in it for a distance of three miles would be taken in a few hours.

The fish were generally cooked by roasting on hot coals from burned oak wood or bark.

ACORNS AS FOOD.

Acorns were their main staple article of breadstuff, and they are still used by the present generation whenever they can be obtained.

CHUCK´-AH.

Storehouse for nuts and acorns, thatched with pine branches, points downward, to keep out mice and squirrels.

They are gathered in the fall when ripe and are preserved for future use in the old style Indian *cache* or storehouse. This consists of a structure which they call a *chuck´-ah*, which is a large basket-shaped receptacle made of long willow sprouts closely woven together. It is usually about six feet high and three feet in diameter. It is set upon stout posts about three feet high and supported in position by four longer posts on the outside, reaching to the top, and there bound firmly to keep them from spreading. The outside of the basket is thatched with small pine branches, points downward, to shed the rain and snow, and to protect the contents from the depredations of squirrels and woodpeckers. When filled, the top also is securely covered with bark, as a protection from the winter storms. When the acorns are wanted for use, a small hole is made at the bottom of the *chuck´-ah*, and they are taken out from time to time as required.

The acorns from the black or Kellogg's oak (*Quercus Californica*) are considered much the best and most nutritious by the Indians. This is the oak which is so beautiful and abundant in the Yosemite Valley.

These acorns are quite bitter, and are not eaten in their natural condition, as most fruit and nuts are eaten, but have to be quite elaborately prepared and cooked to make them palatable. First, the hull is cracked and removed, and the kernel pounded or ground into a fine meal. In the Yosemite Valley and at other Indian camps in the mountains, this is done by grinding with their stone pestles or *metats (may-tat´s)* in the *ho´yas* or mortars, worn by long usage in large flat-top granite rocks, one of which is near every Indian camp. Lower down in the foothills, where there are no suitable large rocks for these permanent mortars, the Indians used single portable stone mortars for this purpose.

HO´-YAS AND ME-TATS´.

Rude mortars and pestles for grinding acorn meal. The holes have been worn in the granite by constant use.

After the acorns are ground to a fine meal, the next process is to take out the bitter tannin principle. This is done in the following manner: They make large shallow basins in clean washed sand, in the center of which are laid a few flat, fan-like ends of fir branches. A fire is then made near by, and small stones of four or five pounds in weight are heated, with which they warm water in some of their large cooking baskets, and mix the acorn meal with it to the consistency of thin gruel. This mixture is poured into the sand basins, and as the water leaches out into the sand it takes with it the bitter quality—the warm water being renewed until all the bitter taste is washed out from the meal sediment, or dough.

This is then taken, and, after being cleansed from the adhering sand, is put into cooking baskets, thinned down with hot water to the desired condition, and cooked by means of hot stones which are held in it with two sticks for tongs. The mush, while cooking, is stirred with a peculiar stirring stick, made of a tough oak sprout, doubled so as to form a round, open loop at one end, which is used in lifting out any loose stones. When the dough is well cooked, it is either left *en masse* in the basket or scooped out in rolls and put into cold water to cool and warden before being eaten. Sometimes the thick paste is made into cakes and baked on hot rocks. One of these cakes, when rolled in paper, will in a short time saturate it with oil. This acorn food is probably more nutritious than any of the cereals.

INDIAN DOGS.

The Indian dogs, of which every family had several, are as fond of the acorn food as their owners. These dogs are made useful in treeing wild-cats, California lions and gray squirrels, and are very expert in catching ground squirrels by intercepting them when away from their burrows, and when the Indians drown them out in the early spring by turning water from the flooded streams into their holes.

As far as can be learned, dogs were about the only domestic animals which the Yosemites, and other adjacent tribes of Indians, kept for use before the country was settled by the white people.

NUTS AND BERRIES.

Pine nuts were another important article of food, and were much prized by the Indians. They are very palatable and nutritious, and are also greatly relished by white people whenever they can be obtained. The seeds of the Digger or nut pine (*Pinus Sabiniana*) were the ones most used on the western side of the Sierras, although the seeds of the sugar pine (*P. Lambertiana*) were also sometimes eaten. On account of their soft shell, nuts from the pinon pine (*P. monophylla*), which grows principally on the eastern side of the mountains, were considered superior to either of the other kinds, and were an important article of barter with the tribes of that region. All of these trees are very prolific, and their crop of nuts in fruitful years has been estimated to be even greater than the enormous wheat crop of California, although of course but a very small portion of it is ever gathered. Many other kinds of nuts and seeds were also eaten.

The principal berries used by the Indians of Yosemite and tribes lower down in the foothills were those of the manzanita (*Arctostaphylos glauca*). They are about the size of huckleberries, of a light brown color, and when ripe have the flavor of dried apples. They are used for eating, and also to make a kind of cider for drinking, and for mixing with some food preparations. Manzanita is the Spanish for "little apple," and this shrub, with its rich red bark and pale green foliage, is perhaps the most beautiful and most widely distributed in California. Strawberries, black raspberries, elderberries, wild cherries and the fruit of the Sierra plum (*Prunus subcordata*) are also used by the Indians, but wild edible berries are not as plentiful in California as they are in the Atlantic States.

GRASSHOPPERS AND WORMS.

In addition to the staple articles of food already mentioned, many other things were eaten when they could be obtained. These included grasshoppers, certain kinds of large tree worms, the white fungi which grows upon the oak, mushrooms, and the larvae and pupae of ants and other insects. The pupae of a certain kind of fly which breeds extensively on the shores of Mono Lake, about forty miles from Yosemite, was an important article of commerce across the mountains, and was made into a kind of paste called *ka-cha´-vee*, which is still much relished by the Indians, and is a prominent dish at their feasts.

The manner of catching grasshoppers was to dig a large hole, somewhat in the shape of a fly trap, with the bottom larger than the opening at the top, so that the insects could not readily get out of it. This hole was dug in the center of a meadow, which was then surrounded by Indians armed with small boughs, who beat the grasshoppers towards a common center and drove them into the trap. A fire was then kindled on top of them, and after they had been well roasted they were gathered up and stored for future use.

50

A WOOD GATHERER.

As in all Indian tribes, the women do most of the work.

Other articles of food were various kinds of roots, grasses and herbage, some of which were cooked, while others were eaten in their natural condition. The lupine (*Lupinus bicolor* and other species), whose brilliant flowers are such a beautiful feature of all the mountain meadows in the spring and summer, was a favorite plant for making what white people would call "greens," and when eaten was frequently moistened with some of the manzanita cider already referred to. Among the roots used for food were those of the wild caraway (*Carum*), wild hyacinth (*Brodioea*), sorrel (*Oxalis*), and camass (*Camassia esculenta*).

Chapter Five

RELIGIOUS CEREMONIES AND BELIEFS.

The Indians of this region, in common with most, if not all, of the North American aborigines, were of a highly religious temperament, most devout in their beliefs and observances, and easily wrought upon by the priests or medicine men of their tribes. Elaborate ceremonies were carried out, in which all of the details were highly symbolical, and some of their curious and picturesque superstitions were responsible for acts of cruelty and vengeance, which in many cases were foreign to their natural disposition.

DANCES.

Dancing was an important part of all religious observances, and was practiced purely as a ceremonial, and never for pleasure or recreation. Both men and women took part, the men executing a peculiar shuffling step which involved a great deal of stamping upon the ground with their bare feet, and the women performing a curious sideways, swaying motion. Some of the dancers carried wands or arrows, and indulged in wild gesticulations. They usually circled slowly around a fire, and danced to the point of exhaustion, when others would immediately take their places. The ceremony was accompanied by the beating of rude drums, and by a monotonous chant, which was joined in by all the dancers.

The great occasions for dancing were before going to war, and when cremating the bodies of their dead. The war dance was probably the most elaborate in costume and other details, and of recent years the Indians have sometimes given public exhibitions of what purported to be war dances, but these performances, like everything else which they do from purely mercenary motives, are very poor imitations of the originals, and it is doubtful if they have ever allowed a genuine war dance to be witnessed by white men.

FESTIVALS.

The various tribes in the vicinity of Yosemite Valley are accustomed to hold a great meeting or festival once a year, each tribe taking its turn as hosts, and the others sometimes coming from considerable distances. At these meetings there are dances and other ceremonials, and also a grand feast, for which extensive preparations are made. Another feature of the occasion is the presentation of gifts to the visiting tribes, consisting of money, blankets, clothing, baskets, bead-work, or other valuable articles. These presents, or their equivalent, no matter how small they may be, are always returned to the givers at the next annual festival, together with additional gifts, which, in turn, must be given back the following year, and so on.

At these gatherings an Indian is appointed to secure and keep on hand a good supply of wood for the camp fires, and every day he spreads a blanket on the ground and sits on it, and the other Indians throw money, clothing, or other contributions, into the blanket, to pay him and his assistants for their services. At other times this man acts as a messenger or news carrier—first spreading his blanket to collect his fees, and then starting off on his mission.

MARRIAGE.

Many of the Indians in Mariposa and adjoining counties were polygamists, having two or three, and sometimes more, wives. Some of the chiefs and head men would have wives from several of the adjacent tribes, which had a tendency to establish permanent friendly relations among them.

Every man who took a young woman for his wife had to buy her. Young women were considered by their parents as personal chattels, subject to sale to the highest suitable bidder, and the payment of the price constituted the main part of the marriage ceremony. The wife was then the personal property of the husband, which he might sell or gamble away if he wished; but such instances were said to be very rare. In case negotiations for a marriage fell through, the preliminary payments were scrupulously returned to the rejected suitor by the parents.

Even a widow, independent of control in the matter of marriage, if she consented to become a man's wife, received some compensation herself from her intended husband.

A YOUNG YOSEMITE.

The babies are tied to their baskets to make them straight, and keep them out of mischief.

It is said that in their marital relations they were as a rule strictly faithful to each other. If the woman was found to be guilty of unfaithfulness to her husband, the penalty was death. Such a thing as a man whipping or beating his wife was never known. Whipping under any circumstances was considered a more humiliating and disgraceful punishment than death.

Even in the management of children, whipping was never resorted to as punishment for disobedience. In fact, children were always treated in such a kind, patient, loving manner, that disobedience was a fault rarely known. The pre-natal maternal influence, and subsequent treatment after birth, were such that they were naturally patient and readily submissive to kind parental control.

In recent years, under the influence and examples often seen in what is called civilized life, Indian husbands have been known to beat their wives, and mothers to whip their children.

LENA AND VIRGIL.

The canopy of the baby basket is called Cho-ko´-ni and the Royal Arches, from their resemblance to it, have also received this name from the Indians.

MEDICINE MEN.

At the time of the settlement of California by the whites, every Indian tribe had its professional doctors or medicine men, who also acted as religious leaders. They were the confidential counselors of the chiefs and head-men of the tribes, and had great influence and control over the people. They claimed to be spiritual mediums, and to have communication with the departed spirits of some of their old and most revered chieftains and dear friends, now in a much more happy condition than when here in earthly life. They were thought to be endowed with supernatural powers, not only in curing all diseases (except those due to old age), but also in making a well person sick at their pleasure, even at a distance; but when their sorcery failed to work on their white enemies and exterminate them, they lost the confidence of their followers to a large extent.

With the invasion of the white settlers came forced changes in their old customs and manner of living, and a new variety of epidemic and other diseases. When a doctor failed to cure these diseases, and several deaths occurred in quick succession in a camp, they believed the doctor was under the control of some evil spirit, and killed him.

After the Indians were given their freedom from the reservations in 1855, the old ones, subdued and broken-hearted, sickened and died very fast, and most of the men doctors were killed off in a few years. There are none known who now attempt to act in that capacity.

There are still some women doctors who continue to practice the magic art, but as there are now but very few Indians, there is not so much sickness, and very few deaths in a year, so that the doctors very rarely forfeit their lives by many of their patients dying in quick succession.

Their most common mode of treatment in cases of sickness was to scarify the painful locality with the sharp edge of a piece of obsidian, and suck out the blood with the mouth. In cases of headache, the forehead was operated on; in a case of colic the abdomen was treated in the same way, as were also all painful swellings on any part of the body.

The grand object of the doctor was to make the patient and family firmly believe that his course of treatment was removing the cause of the sickness. To aid in strengthening this belief, after diagnosing the case, and before commencing operations, he would quietly retire for a short time, ostensibly to get under the influence of the divine healing spirit, but in reality to fill his mouth with several small articles, such as bits of wood or stone; he was then ready to commence treatment. After sucking and spitting pure blood a few times, he began to spit out with the blood, one after another, the things he had in his mouth, at the sight of which all the attendants would join in a chorus of grunts of astonishment, and the doctor would pretend to be very much nauseated. In most ordinary cases two or three treatments effected a cure.

The doctors also made use of certain rare medicinal plants in treating some diseases. The Indian women have great faith in charms made of the pungent roots of some rare plants from the high mountain ranges, which they wear on strings around their necks, or on a string of beads, to protect them from sickness.

In cases of malignant sores or ulcers on any part of the body, the doctors treated them by applying dirt or earth, and in warm weather would excavate a place in the ground and put the patient in it, either in a sitting or recumbent position, as the nature of the case required, and cover the affected part with earth for several hours, daily. Sometimes, by this mode of treatment, wonderful cures were made.

In all cases, if a doctor failed to cure a disease, and the patient died, he was obliged to refund to the relatives any fee which he had received for his services.

DISPOSING OF THE DEAD.

In the early days of the settlement of California, it seemed to be the universal custom of the Indians along the foothills of the Sierra Nevada range of mountains to burn the bodies of their dead.

A suitable pile of readily combustible wood was prepared. The body was taken charge of by persons chosen to perform the last sacred rites, and firmly bound in skins or blankets, and then placed upon the funeral pyre, with all the personal effects of the deceased, together with numerous votive offerings from friends and relatives. The chief mourners of the occasion seemed to take but little active part in the ceremonies. When all was ready, one of the assistants would light the fire, and the terrible, wailing, mournful cry would commence, and the professional chanters, with peculiar sidling movements and frantic gestures, would circle round and round about the burning pile. Occasionally, on arriving at the northwest corner of the pile, they would stop, and, pointing to the West, would end a crying refrain by exclaiming "*Him-i-la´-ha!*" When these became exhausted, others would step in and take their places, and thus keep up the mournful ceremony until the whole pile was consumed.

After the pile had cooled, the charred bones and ashes were gathered up, a few pieces of bone selected, and the remainder buried. Of the pieces retained, some would be sent to distant relatives, and the others pounded to a fine powder, then mixed with pine pitch and plastered on the faces of the nearest female relatives as a badge of mourning, to be kept there until it naturally wore off. Every Indian camp used to have some of these hideous looking old women in it in the "early days."

One principal reason for burning the bodies of the dead was the belief that there is an evil spirit, waiting and watching for the animating spirit or soul to leave the body, that he may get it to take to his own world of darkness and misery. By burning the perishable body they thought that the immortal soul would be more quickly released and set free to speed to the happy spirit world in the *El-o´-win*, or far distant West, while with their loud, wailing cries the evil spirit was kept away.

The young women take great care of their long, shiny, black hair, of which they all feel very proud, as adding much to their personal beauty, and they seldom have it cut before marriage. But upon the death of a husband the wife has her hair all cut off and burned with his body, so that he may still have it in his future spirit home, to love and caress as a memento of his living earth-wife.

Photograph by Boysen.

OLD KALAPINE.

One of the oldest Indians in the Valley. The short hair is a badge of widowhood.

These Indians believe that everything on earth, both natural and artificial, is endowed with an immortal spirit, which is indestructible, and that whatever personal property or precious gifts are burned, either with the body or in later years for the departed friend's benefit, will be received and made use of in the spirit world. In recent years the Yosemites and other remnants of tribes closely associated with them, have adopted the custom of the white people, and bury their dead. The fine, expensive blankets, and most beautifully worked baskets, which have been kept sacredly in hiding for many years, to be buried with the owner, are now cut into small fragments before being deposited in the ground, for fear some white person will desecrate the grave by digging them up and carrying them away.

There are no people in the world who more reverence for their dead, or hold memory more sacred, than these so-called "Digger" Indians. After being released from the reservations they kept themselves in abject poverty for many sacrificing their best blankets, baskets and clothing in the devouring flames of a fire kindled for that purpose, when holding their annual mourning festivals in memory of their dead friends.

RELIGIOUS BELIEFS.

The old Indians are all very reticent regarding their religious beliefs. They hold them too sacred to be exposed to possible ridicule, and it is therefore very difficult to get information from them by direct questions.

They seem, however, to have a vague, indistinct belief or tradition that their original ancestors, in the long forgotten past, dwelt in a better and much more desirable country than this, in the *El-o´-win*, or distant West, and that by some misfortune or great calamity they were separated from that nappy land, and became wanderers in this part of the world. They also believe that the spirits of all good Indians will be permitted, after death, to go back to that happy country of their ancestors' origin; but that the spirits of bad Indians have to serve another earth life in the form of a grizzly bear, as a punishment for their former crimes. Hence, no Indians ever eat bear meat if they know it.

All the old Indians are spiritualists, and very superstitious in their religious beliefs. One special tenet is that if one of their relatives or friends has been murdered, he will not receive them on terms of friendship in the spirit world unless they revenge his death, by either killing the murderer or some one of the same blood. This belief sometimes results in an entirely innocent person being put to death.

They all have a great fear of evil spirits, which they believe have the power to do them much harm and defeat their undertakings. They also have a fairly distinct idea of a Diety or Great Spirit, who never does them any harm, and whose home is in the happy land of their ancestors in the West.

Photograph by Boysen.

YOSEMITE BASKETRY.

The Ellen Boysen collection of baskets and bead work.

Chapter Six

NATIVE INDUSTRIES.

The Yosemites and other kindred or adjacent tribes have been branded as "Diggers," and are generally thought to be the lowest class of Indians in America, but in some lines of artistic work they excelled all other tribes. For example, their basketry work, for domestic and sacred purposes, and their bows and arrows, were of very superior workmanship and fine finish.

BASKETRY AND BEAD WORK.

Many years ago the chief industry of the Indian women, aside from their other domestic duties, was the making of baskets. They made a great variety of shapes and sizes for their common use, and also many of a more artistic design and finer finish for the sacred purpose of being burned or buried with their bodies, or that of some relative or dear friend, after death. The baskets devoted to this special purpose are the finest made, but are very seldom seen by any white person, and are not for sale at any price. This finest style of work seems to have been made a specialty by certain of the most artistic workers in each tribe.

MRS. JORGENSEN'S COLLECTION OF BASKETS.

For the mythical origin of basket-making in the Yosemite see "Legend of To-tau-kon-nu´-la and Tis-sa´-ack."

At the present time, in their more modern style of living, they do not require so many baskets, and the industry of making them is fast on the decline. Some of the old women, however, still continue to make such as are required for their own use, and a few others for sale.

Most of the ornamental figures and designs worked into the finest basketry are symbolical in character, and of so ancient an origin that Indians of the present day do not know what many of them are intended to represent. They have simply been copied from time immemorial, with the idea that they were necessary for the complete finish and beauty of the article made.

In recent years they sometimes make use of more modern styles of ornamentation, which they see in print.

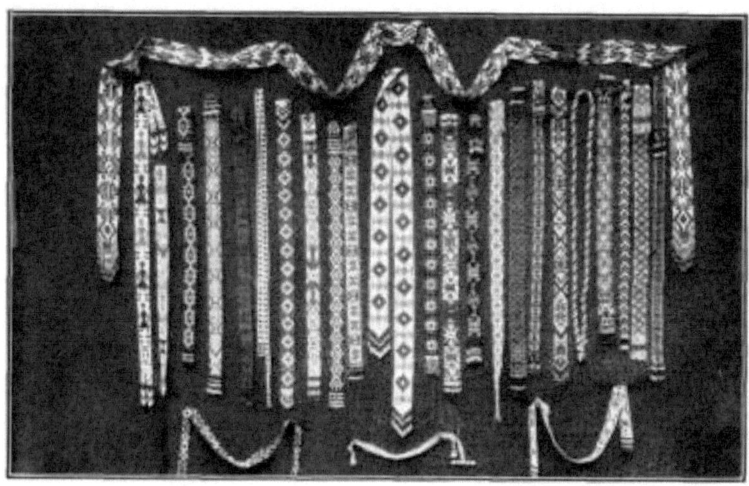

Photograph by Fiske.

INDIAN BEAD WORK.

Mrs. George Fiske's collection of Yosemite and Pai-ute´ bead work.

Many of the young women are now giving their attention to making fancy bead work, in the form of ornamental belts and hat-bands, but this is an industry of very modern origin. Some of them are employed by white people to do laundry and other work, and any labor of this kind pays them better than making baskets for sale. Forty years ago a finely made basket could have been bought for less than ten dollars. At present, if the time spent in getting and preparing the necessary materials, and in working them into the basket, were paid for at the same rate per day that a young woman receives for doing washing in the hotel laundry, or for private families, it would amount to over one hundred dollars.

Most of the baskets made for domestic use are so closely woven that they are practically water-tight, and are used for cooking and similar purposes. Over on the eastern side of the Sierra Nevada Mountains, near the dry, desert country, the Indians make some of their baskets in the form of jugs of various sizes. These are smeared over with a pitch composition, which renders them perfectly water-tight, and they are used for carrying water when traveling over those desolate, sandy wastes.

BOWS AND ARROWS.

The Indian men showed no less ingenuity artistic skill in their special lines of work than the women, especially in manufacture of their bows and arrows, in the making of fish lines and coarser twine out of the soft, flexible bark of the milkweed (*Asclepias speciosa*), and in making other useful implements and utensils with the very limited means at their disposal.

Their bows were made of a branch of the incense cedar (*Libocedrus decurrens*), or of the California nutmeg (*Tumion Californicum [Torreya]*), made flat on the outer side, and rounded smooth on the inner or concave side when the bow is strung for use. The flat, outer side was covered with sinew, usually that from the leg of a deer, steeped in hot water until it became soft and glutinous, and then laid evenly and smoothly over the wood, and so shaped at the ends as to hold the string in place. When thoroughly dry the sinew contracted, so that the bow when not strung was concave on the outer side.

Photograph by Boysen.

A BASKET MAKER.

She is weaving a burden basket. The one to the left is for cooking, and a baby basket stands against the tent.

When not in use the bow was always left unstrung. To string it for use, it was necessary in cold weather to warm it, thus making it more elastic and easily bent. The best strings were also made of sinew, or of pax-wax cartilage, for their finest bows.

The arrows were made of reeds and various kinds of wood, including the syringa (*Philadelphus Lewisii*) and a small shrub or tree which the Indians called *Le-ham´-i-tee*, or arrow-wood, and which grew quite plentifully in what is now known as Indian Canyon, near the Yosemite Falls.

The finest arrows were furnished with points made of obsidian, or volcanic glass, which was obtained in the vicinity of Mono Lake on the eastern side of the Sierras. It required great care and delicate skill to work this brittle material into the fine sharp points, and the making of them seemed to be a special business or trade with some of the old men. Arrows furnished with these points were only used in hunting large game, or in hostile combat with enemies; for common use, in hunting small game, the hard wooden arrow was merely sharpened to a point.

The butt, or end used on the string, was furnished with three or four short strips of feathers taken from a hawk's wing, and fastened on lengthwise. These strips of feathers are supposed to aid in the more accurate flight of the arrow when shot from the bow.

When out on a hunt the Indian carried his bow strung ready for use, and his bundle of assorted arrows in a quiver made of the skin of a small fox, wild-cat or fisher, hung conveniently over his shoulder.

These primitive weapons, which were in universal use by the Yosemite Indians fifty years ago, are now never seen except in some collection of Indian relics and curios.

Other articles manufactured by these tribes were stone hammers, and also others made from the points of deer horns mounted on wooden handles, which they used in delicately chipping the brittle obsidian in forming arrowheads. Rude musical instruments, principally drums and flageolets, were also made.

Chapter Seven.

MYTHS AND LEGENDS.

The Indians of the Yosemite Valley and vicinity have a great fund of mythological lore, which has been handed down verbally from generation to generation for hundreds of years, but they are very reluctant to speak of these legends to white people, and it is extremely difficult to get reliable information on the subject. Moreover, the Indians most familiar with them have not a sufficient knowledge of the English language to be able to express their ideas clearly.

Many Yosemite legends have been published at different times and in various forms, and it is probable that most of them have had at least a foundation in real Indian myths, but many are obviously fanciful in some particulars, and it is impossible to tell how much is of Indian origin and how much is due to poetic embellishment. When asked about some of these legends, many years ago, one of the old Yosemite Indians remarked contemptuously, "White man too much lie."

On the other hand, red men as well as white men are sometimes given to romancing, and I have known of cases where "legends" would be manufactured on the spur of the moment by some young Indian to satisfy an importunate and credulous questioner, to the keen but suppressed amusement of other Indians present.

It will therefore be seen that this subject is surrounded with some difficulty, and it must not be understood that the legends here given are vouched for as of wholly Indian origin. Some of them, notably those of the Tul-tok´-a-na and the second legend of Tis-sa´-ack, have been accepted by eminent ethnologists, and are believed to be purely aboriginal, while others have doubtless been somewhat idealized in translation and in the course of numerous repetitions.

The legend of To-tau-kon-nu´-la and Tis-sa´-ack is made up of fragments of mythological lore obtained from a number of old Indians at various times during the past fifty years. It varies somewhat from other legends which have been published regarding these same characters, but it is well known that the Indians living in Yo-semite in recent years are of mixed tribal origin and do not all agree as to the traditional history of the region, nor the names of the prominent scenic features, nor even of the Valley itself. And this largely accounts for the fact that some of the legends do not harmo-nize with each other in details or in sentiment. All of them, howev-er, are picturesque, and they certainly give an added interest to the natural beauties and wonders with which they are associated.

LEGEND OF TO-TAU-KON-NU´-LA AND TIS-SA´-ACK.

Innumerable moons and snows have passed since the Great Spirit guided a little band of his favorite children into the beautiful vale of Ah-wah´-nee [Yosemite Valley], and bid them stop and rest from their long and weary wanderings, which had lasted ever since they had been separated by the great waters from the happy land of their forefathers in the far distant *El-o´-win* (West).

MARY.

Daughter of Captain John, one of the last Chiefs of the Yosemites.

Here they found food in abundance for all. The rivers gave them plenty of *la-pe´-si* (trout). They found in the meadows sweet *ha´-ker* (clover), and sour *yu-yu-yu-mah* (oxalis) for spring medicine, and sweet *toon´-gy* and other edible roots in abundance. The trees and bushes yielded acorns, pine nuts, fruits and berries. In the forests were herds of *he´-ker* (deer) and other animals, which gave meat for food and skins for clothing and beds. And here they lived and multiplied, and, as instructed by their medicine men, worshipped the Great Spirit which gave them life, and the sun which warmed and made them happy.

They also kept in memory the happy land of their forefathers. The story was told by the old people to the young, and they again told it to their children from generation to generation, and they all believed that after death their spirits would return to dwell forever in that distant country.

They prospered and built other towns outside of Ah-wah´-nee, and became a great nation. They learned wisdom by experience and by observing how the Great Spirit taught the animals and insects to live, and they believed that their children could absorb the cunning of the wild creatures. And so the young son of their chieftain was made to sleep in the skins of the beaver and coyote, that he might grow wise in building, and keen of scent in following game. On some days he was fed with *la-pe´-si* that he might become a good swimmer, and on other days the eggs of the great *to-tau´-kon* (crane) were his food, that he might grow tall and keen of sight, and have a clear, ringing voice. He was also fed on the flesh of the *he´-ker* that he might be fleet of foot, and on that of the great *yo-sem´-i-te* (grizzly bear) to make him powerful in combat.

And the little boy grew up and became a great and wise chieftain, and he was also a rain wizard, and brought timely rains for the crops.

As was the custom in giving names to all Indians, his name was changed from time to time, as his character developed, until he was called Choo´-too-se-ka´, meaning the Supreme Good. His grand *o-chum* (house) was built at the base of the great rock called To-tau-kon-nu´-la [El Capitan], because the great *to-tau´-kons* made their nests and raised their young in a meadow at its summit, and their loud ringing cries resounded over the whole Valley.

As the moons and snows passed, this great rock and all the great rocky walls around the Valley grew in height, and the hills became high mountains.

After a time Choo´-too-se-ka´ built himself a great palace *o´-chum* on the summit of the rock To-tau-kon-nu´-la, and had his great chair of state a little west of his palace, where on all festival occasions he could overlook and talk to the great multitude below; and the remains of this chair are still to be seen.

Choo´-too-se-ka´ was then named To-tau-kon-nu´-la, because he had built his *o´-chum* on the summit of the great rock and taken the place of the *to-tau´-kons*. He had no wife, but all the women served him in his domestic needs, as he was their great chief, and his wishes were paramount. The many valuable donations which he received from his people at the great annual festivals made him wealthy beyond all personal wants, and he gave freely to the needy.

One day, while standing on the top of the great dome [Sentinel Dome] above the south wall of the Valley, watching the great herds of deer, he saw some strange people approaching, bearing heavy burdens. They were fairer of skin, and their clothing was different from that of his people, and when they drew near he asked them who they were and whence they came.

And a woman replied, "I am Tis-sa´-ack, and these are some of my people. We come from *cat´-tan chu´-much* (far South). I have heard of your great wisdom and goodness, and have come to see you and your people. We bring you presents of many fine baskets, and beads of many colors, as tokens of our friendship. When we have rested and seen your people and beautiful valley we will return to our home."

HALF DOME (TIS-SA´-ACK). 5,000 Feet.

Named for a woman in Indian mythology who was turned to stone for quarreling with her husband. See "Legend of Tis-sa´-ack."

To-tau-kon-nu´-la was much pleased with his fair visitor, and built a large *o´-chum* for her and her companions on the summit of the great dome at the east end of the Valley [Half Dome], and this dome still retains her name.

And she tarried there and taught the women of Ah-wah´-nee how to make the beautiful baskets which they still make at the present day; and To-tau-kon-nu´-la visited her daily, and became charmed with her loveliness, and wanted her to remain and be his wife, but she denied him, saying, "I must return to my people," and, when he still persisted, she left her *o´-chum* in the night and was never seen again. And the love-stricken chieftain forgot his people, and went in search of her, and they waited many moons for his return and mourned his long absence, but they never saw him more.

This was the beginning of a series of calamities which nearly destroyed the great tribe of Ah-wah-nee´-chees. First a great drouth prevailed, and the crops failed, and the streams of water dried up. The deer went wild and wandered away. Then a dark cloud of smoke arose in the East and obscured the sun, so that it gave no heat, and many of the people perished from cold and hunger. Then the earth shook terribly and groaned with great pain, and enormous rocks fell from the walls around Ah-wah´-nee. The great dome called Tis-sa´-ack was burst asunder, and half of it fell into the Valley. A fire burst out of the earth in the East, and the *ca´-lah* (snow) on the sky mountains was changed to water, which flowed down and formed the Lake Ah-wei´-yah [Mirror Lake]. And all the streams were filled to overflowing, and still the waters rose, and there was a great flood, so that a large part of the Valley became a lake, and many persons were drowned.

After a time the Great Spirit took pity on his children, and the dark cloud of smoke disappeared, the sun warmed the Valley again into new life, and the few people who were left had plenty of food once more.

Many moons afterwards there appeared on the face of the great rock To-tau-kon-nu´-la the figure of a man in a flowing robe, and with one hand extended toward the West, in which direction he appears to be traveling. This figure was interpreted to be the picture of the great lost Chieftain, indicating that he had gone to the "happy hunting grounds" of his ancestors, and it is looked upon with great veneration and awe by the few Indians still living in Yosemite.

At about the same time the face of the beautiful Tis-sa´-ack appeared on the great flat side of the dome which bears her name, and the Indians recognized her by the way in which her dark hair was cut straight across her forehead and fell down at the sides, which was then considered among the Yosemites as the acme of feminine beauty, and is so regarded to this day.

Photograph by Fiske

A BURDEN BEARER.

The women are the principal burden bearers and all loads are carried in large baskets, supported by a band across the forehead.

ANOTHER LEGEND OF TIS-SA´-ACK.

Tis-sa´-ack and her husband traveled from a far-off country, and entered the Valley footsore and weary. She walked ahead, carrying a great conical burden-basket, which was supported by a band across her forehead, and was filled with many things. He followed after, carrying a rude staff in his hand and a roll of woven skin blankets over his shoulder. They had come across the mountains and were very thirsty, and they hurried to reach the Valley, where they knew there was water. The woman was still far in advance when she reached the Lake Ah-wei´-yah [Mirror Lake], and she dipped up the water in her basket and drank long and deep. She was so thirsty that she even drank up all the water in the lake and drained it dry before her husband arrived. And because the lake was dry there came a terrible drouth in the Valley, and the soil was dried up and nothing grew.

And the husband was much displeased because the woman had drunk up all the water and left none for him, and he became so angry that he forgot the customs of his people and beat the woman with his staff. She ran away from him, but he followed her and beat her yet more. And she wept, and in her anger she turned and reviled her husband, and threw her basket at him. And while they were in this attitude, one facing the other, they were turned into stone for their wickedness, and there they still retain. The upturned basket lies beside the husband, where the woman threw it, and the woman's face is tear stained with long dark lines trailing down.

Half-Dome is the woman Tis-sa´-ack and North Dome is her husband, while beside the latter is a smaller dome which is still called Basket Dome to this day.

LEGEND OF THE GRIZZLY BEAR.

The significance and derivation of the name "Yosemite," as given by old Tenei´-ya, chief of the tribe, have been explained in another chapter, but there is also a legendary account of its origin, which may be of interest.

Long, long ago, when the remote ancestors of the Yosemite Indians dwelt peacefully in the valley called Ah-wah´-nee [Yosemite Valley], one of the stalwart young braves of the tribe went early one

morning to spear some fish in the lake Ah-wei´-yah [Mirror Lake].
Before reaching his destination he was confronted by a huge grizzly
bear, who appeared from behind one of the enormous boulders in
that vicinity, and savagely disputed his passage.

EL CAPITAN (TO-TAU-KON-NU´-LA), 3,300 Feet.

Indians believe that this great rock grew from a small boulder. See "Legend of the Tul-tok´-a-na."

Being attacked in this unexpected manner, the Indian defended himself to the best of his ability, using for the purpose the dead limb of a tree which was near at hand, and, after a long and furious struggle, in which he was badly wounded, he at length succeeded in killing the bear.

His exploit was considered so remarkable by the rest of the tribe that they called him Yo-sem´-i-te (meaning a full-grown grizzly bear), in honor of his achievement, and this name was transmitted to his children, and eventually to the whole tribe.

LEGEND OF THE TUL-TOK´-A-NA.

There were once two little boys living in the Valley of Ah-wah´-nee, who went down to the river to swim. When they had finished their bath they went on shore and lay down on a large boulder to dry themselves in the sun. While lying there they fell asleep, and slept so soundly that they never woke up again. Through many moons and many snows they slept, and while they slept the great rock [El Capitan] on which they lay was slowly rising, little by little, until it soon lifted them up out of sight, and their friends searched for them everywhere without success. Thus they were carried up into the blue sky, until they scraped their faces against the moon; and still they slept on.

NORTH DOME (TO-KO´-YA). 3,725 Feet.

This rock is believed by the Indians to represent Tis-sa´-ack's husband, turned into stone for beating his wife. The lower dome to the right is the basket which she threw at him. See "Legend of Tis-sa´-ack."

Then all the animals assembled to bring down the little boys from the top of the great rock. Each animal sprang up the face of the rock as far as he could. The mouse could only spring a hand's breadth, the rat two hands' breadths, the raccoon a little more, and so on. The grizzly bear made a great leap up the wall, but fell back like all the others, without reaching the top. Finally came the lion, who jumped up farther than any of the others, but even he fell back and could not reach the top.

Then came the *tul-tok´-a-na,* the insignificant measuring worm, who was despised by all the other creatures, and began to creep up the face of the rock. Step by step, little by little, he measured his way up until he was soon above the lion's jump, and still farther and farther, until presently he was out of sight; and still he crawled up and up, day and night, through many moons, and at length he reached the top, and took the little boys and brought them safely down to the ground. And therefore the rock was named for the measuring worm, and was called Tu-tok-a-nu´-la.

LEGEND OF GROUSE LAKE.

I will here relate a personal experience which occurred in September, 1857, while out with a large party of Indians on a deer hunt in the mountains.

One day, after a long tramp, I stopped to rest by the side of a small lake about eight miles from the present site of Wawona, and I then named it Grouse Lake on account of the great number of grouse found there. Very soon a party of Indians came along carrying some deer, and stopped on the opposite side of the lake to rest and get some water. Soon after they had started again for their camp I heard a distinct wailing cry, somewhat like the cry of a puppy when lost, and I thought the Indians must have left one of their young dogs behind.

When I joined the Indians in camp that night I inquired of them about the sound I had heard. They replied that it was not a dog—that a long time ago an Indian boy had been drowned in the lake, and that every time any one passed there he always cried after them, and that no one dared to go in the lake, for he would catch them by the legs and pull them down and they would, be drowned. I then concluded that it must have been some unseen water-fowl that made the cry, and at that time I thought that the Indians were trying to impose on my credulity, but I am now convinced that they fully believed the story they told me.

Po-ho´-no Lake, the headwaters of the Bridal Veil Creek, was also thought to be haunted by troubled spirits, which affected the stream clear down into the Yosemite Valley; and the Indians believed that an evil wind there had been the cause of some fatal accidents many years ago. The word Po-ho´-no means a puffing wind, and has also been translated "Evil Wind," on account of the superstition above referred to.

LEGEND OF THE LOST ARROW.

Tee-hee´-nay was a beautiful Ah-wah´-nee maiden, said to be the most beautiful of her tribe, and she was beloved by Kos-su´-kah, a strong and valiant young brave. Valuable presents had been made to the bride's parents, and they had given their consent to an early marriage, which was to be celebrated by a great feast.

To provide an abundance of venison and other meat for this banquet, Kos-su´-kah gathered together his young companions and went into the mountains in search of game. In order that Tee-hee´-nay might know of his welfare and the success of the hunt, it was agreed between the lovers that at sunset Kos-su´-kah should go to the high rock to the east of Cho´-lak [Yosemite Falls], and should shoot an arrow into the Valley, to which should be attached a number of grouse feathers corresponding to the number of deer that had fallen before the skill of the hunters.

82

BRIDAL VEIL FALL (PO-HO´-NO). 940 Feet.

The source of this stream is supposed by the Indians to be haunted
by troubled spirits, which affect the water along its whole course.
The word Po-ho´-no means a "puffing wind."

At the time appointed Tee-hee´-nay went near the foot of the
great cliff and waited, with her eyes raised to the towering rocks
above, hoping with her keen sight to see the form of her lover out-
lined against the sky, but no form could she see, and no arrow fell
into the Valley. As darkness gathered, gloomy forebodings took
possession of her, and she climbed part way up the canyon called
Le-ham´-i-tee [now known as Indian Canyon] because the arrow-
wood grew there, and finally she stood at the very foot of the rocky
wall which rose to dizzy heights above her, and there she waited
through the long night.

With the first streak of dawn she bounded swiftly up the rough
canyon, for she was fully convinced that some terrible fate had
overtaken the brave Kos-su´-kah, and soon she stood upon the lofty
summit [Yosemite Point], where she found her lover's footsteps
leading towards the edge of the precipice. Drawing nearer she was
startled to find that a portion of the cliff had given way, and, upon
peering over the brink, what was her horror to discover the blood-
stained and lifeless body of Kos-su´-kah lying on a rocky ledge far
beneath.

Summoning assistance by means of a signal fire, which was seen
from the Valley below, a rope was made of sapling tamaracks
lashed firmly together with thongs from one of the deer that was to
have furnished the marriage feast, and Tee-hee´-nay herself insisted
on being lowered over the precipice to recover the body of her lover. This was at last successfully accomplished, and when his ghastly
form lay once more upon the rocky summit, she threw herself on
his bosom and gave way to passionate outburst of grief.

Finally she became quiet, but when they stooped to raise her they
found that her spirit had fled to join the lost Kos-su´-kah and that
the lovers were re-united in death!

The fateful arrow that was the cause of so much sorrow could never be found, and the Indians believe that it was taken away by the spirits of Kos-su´-kah and Tee-hee´-nay. In memory of them, and of this tragedy, the slender spire of rock [sometimes called "The Devil's Thumb"] that rises heavenward near the top of the cliff at this point is known among the Indians as Hum-mo´, or the Lost Arrow.

Appendix.

HINTS TO YOSEMITE VISITORS.

Secure stage seats in advance.

Take only hand baggage, unless for a protracted visit. For a short trip, an outing suit and two or three waists, with a change for evening wear, will be found sufficient. The free baggage allowance on the stage lines is fifty pounds.

Men will find flannel or negligee shirts the most comfortable.

In April, May and June wear warm clothing and take heavy wraps. In July, August and September wear medium clothing, with light wraps. In October and November wear warm clothing, with heavy wraps. The nights are cool at all seasons.

Dusters are always advisable, and ladies should provide some light head covering to protect the hair from dust. Sun bonnets are frequently worn.

Short skirts are most convenient.

Divided skirts are proper for trail trips, as ladies are required to ride astride. Heavy denim for skirt and bloomers is very satisfactory. Such skirts can be hired in the Valley.

Waists of soft material and neutral shades are appropriate. Avoid white.

Something absolutely soft for neckwear will be found a great comfort, both by men and women.

Leggings, stout, comfortable shoes, and heavy, loose gloves, will be found very serviceable.

A soft felt hat is preferable to straw. One that will shade the eyes is best. A cloth traveling cap is the worst thing to wear.

Smoked glasses will sometimes save the wearer a headache.

Except in April, May and November, an umbrella is apt to be a useless encumbrance.

If the skin is sensitive, and one wishes to avoid painful sunburn, the use of a pure cream and soft cloth is preferable to water, and far more efficacious.

A week is the shortest time that should be allowed for a trip to Yosemite. Two weeks are better. The grandeur of the Valley cannot be fully appreciated in a few days. Those not accustomed to staging or mountain climbing should make some allowance in their itineraries for rest. Many visitors spoil their pleasure by getting too tired.

Take a little more money than you think will be needed. You may want to prolong your stay.

Hunting, or the possession of firearms, is not permitted in the Yosemite National Park. Fishing is allowed, and in June and July an expert angler is likely to be well rewarded. Rods and tackle may be hired in the Valley.

There is no hardship, risk or danger in any part of the Yosemite trip. Many old people and children visit the Valley without difficulty.

A knowledge of horsemanship is not needed for going on the trails. The most timid people make the trips with enjoyment. Some of the finest views can only be obtained in this way.

There is a laundry in the Valley.

There is a barber shop.

There is a post office, telegraph and express. There is a general store and places for the sale of photographs, curios and Indian work.

Treat the Indians with courtesy and consideration, if you expect similar treatment from them. Do not expect them to pose for you for nothing. They are asked to do it hundreds of times every summer, and are entitled to payment for their trouble.

Kodak films and plates can be obtained in the Valley.

Developing and printing are done in the Valley.

TAKE YOUR CAMERA.

OFFICIAL TABLE OF DISTANCES AND LIVERY CHARGES.

The following are the legal rates for transportation of tourists in and about the Yosemite Valley:

CARRIAGES.

FROM HOTELS OR PUBLIC Estimated Rate for Rate for CAMPS, AND RETURN. Distance Party of Party of (Round Four or Less Than Trip) More Four Miles Each Each Person Person To Cascades, Yosemite and Bridal Veil Falls 16.00 $1.50 $2.00 To Mirror Lake 5.82 1.00 1.00 To River View and Bridal Veil Falls 10.41 1.00 1.50 To New Inspiration Point 14.38 2.00 2.50 To Happy Isles 4.00 .50 1.00 To Yosemite Falls 3.00 .50 .75

SADDLE HORSES.

FROM HOTELS OR PUBLIC Estimated Rate for Rate for CAMPS, AND RETURN. Distance Party of Party of (Round Four Less Trip) or More Than Four Miles Each Person Each Person To Vernal and Nevada Falls 10.90 $ 2.50 $ 3.00 To Yosemite Falls and Eagle Peak 13.18 3.00 3.00 To Glacier Point and Sentinel Dome 11.14 3.00 3.00 To Yosemite Point 10.00 2.50 3.00 To Eagle Peak 13.00 3.00 3.00 To Vernal and Nevada Falls and Glacier Point (Continuous Trip) 19.22 4.00 5.00 To Glacier Point, Sentinel Dome and Fissures 14.00 3.50 3.75 To Old Inspiration Point and Stanford Point 16.00 4.00 4.00 To Vernal and Nevada Falls and Cloud's Rest (Same Day) 22.00 4.00 5.00 Charges for Guide (Including Horse) When Furnished Free 3.00

1. Trips other than those above specified shall be subject to special arrangements between the parties and the stables.

2. Any excess of the above rates, as well as any extortion, incivility, misrepresentation, or riding of unsafe animals, should be reported to the Superintendent's office.

3. All distances are estimated from the Superintendent's office.

SUPPLEMENTARY TABLE OF DISTANCES.

FROM SUPERINTENDENT'S OFFICE. MILES Bridal Veil Falls 4 Yosemite Falls, base ¾ Upper Yosemite Fall, base 2 ¾ Upper Yosemite Fall, top 4 ¼ Little Yosemite Valley 8 Glacier Point (short trail) 4 ½ Glacier Point (via Nevada Falls) 14 ½ Cascades 8

INTERPRETATION OF INDIAN NAMES.

The Indians had names for all the prominent features of the Yosemite Valley, and these have been variously translated (sometimes with considerable poetic license), and variously spelled. The translations given below are as literal as possible, without embellishment, and are believed to be fairly accurate. The spelling adopted is such as best indicates the pronunciation.

The English names, by which the falls and peaks are commonly known, bear no relation to the Indian names, but were bestowed by the soldiers of the Mariposa Battalion at the time the Valley was discovered. The appropriateness and good taste of most of them are due to Dr. L.H. Bunnell, the surgeon of the expedition.

AH-WAH´-NEE (original name of Yosemite Valley)—"Deep grassy valley."

YO-SEM´-I-TE—"Full-grown grizzly bear."

PO-HO´-NO (Bridal Veil)—"A puffing-wind."

LOI´-YA (The Sentinel)—"A signal station."

CHO´-LACK (Yosemite Falls)—"The falls."

CHO-KO´-NI (Royal Arches)—"Canopy of baby basket." Strictly speaking, this name applies only to a deep alcove near the top of this cliff.

YO-WEI´-YEE (Nevada)—"Twisting."

TO-TAU-KON-NU´-LA (El Capitan)—Named from the To-tau´-kons, or cranes, which used to make their nests in a meadow near the top of this rock.

KU-SO´-KO (Cathedral Rock)—Interpretation doubtful.

PU-SEE´-NA CHUCK´-AH (Cathedral Spires)—"Pu-see-na" means mouse or rat, and might possibly be applied to a squirrel. "Chuck-ah" is a store house or *cache*.

WAW-HAW´-KEE (Three Brothers)—"Falling rocks." Pom-pom-pa´-sus, usually given as the Indian name of the Three Brothers, is the name of a smaller rock immediately to the West.

WEI-YOW´ (Mt. Watkins)—"Juniper Mountain."

TO-KO´-YA (North Dome)—"The Basket."

TIS-SA´-ACK (Half Dome)—A character in Indian mythology.

MAH´-TA (Cap of Liberty)—Said to mean "Martyr Mountain."

PI-WEI´-ACK (Vernal Fall)—Said to mean "Sparkling water."

LE-HAM´-I-TEE (Indian Canyon)—"The place of the arrow-wood."

HUM-MO´ (Devil's Thumb)—"The Lost Arrow."

AH-WEI´-YA (Mirror Lake)—"Quiet Water."

TOO-LOO´-LO-WEI-ACK (Illillouette Fall)—Interpretation doubtful.

WAH´-WO-NAH—"Big Tree." (Now commonly spelled and pronounced Wa-wo´-na.)

HEIGHTS OF YOSEMITE'S WATER-FALLS.

FEET Cascades 700 Bridal Veil 940 Ribbon 3,300 Sentinel 3,270 Yosemite (Upper 1,600 ft.; Lower 400 ft.) 2,634 Royal Arch 2,000 Vernal 350 Nevada 700 Illillouette 500

YOSEMITE'S PEAKS AND DOMES. WITH ALTITUDES ABOVE FLOOR OF VALLEY.

(The Valley Floor is about 4,000 feet above sea level.)

FEET Inspiration Point 1,248 El Capitan 3,300 Cathedral Rock 2,678 Cathedral Spires 1,934 Royal Arches (span) 2,000 The Sentinel 3,100 Sentinel Dome 4,122 Three Brothers 3,900 Eagle Peak 3,900 Yosemite Point 3,220 Glacier Point 3,250 North Dome 3,725 Half Dome 5,000 Cap of Liberty. 3,062 Union Point 2,350 Cloud's Rest. 5,912 Mt. Starr King 5,100

NAMES OF INDIAN NUMERALS.

King-eet´ One O-tee´-cat Two Tul-o´-cat Three O-e´-sart Four Mo´-ho´´-cat Five Te´-mo´´-cat Six Te-tow´-ok Seven Cow-in´-tuk Eight El´-e´´-wok Nine Ne-ah´-jah Ten

Larger numbers are expressed by combinations of these numbers.

INDIAN WORDS IN COMMON USE.

Wat-too´ The Sun Co´-ma Moon He-a´-mah Day Cow-il´-la Night Tum-aw´-lin North Chu´-muck South He´-home East El-o´-win West Het-a-poo´-pa Cold Wool-tut´-tee Hat* Come´-haw Burn Chum´-haw Dead or Die Na´-win Up or Above Hoo´-ya Down or Below Wool-ar´-nee To Hunt or Look For Took´-hah To Kill E´-win Now Oo´-haw By and By Man´-nik More Ut´-tee Much Wa´-le-co Quick Now´-tah To Steal Nung´-hah Man O´-hock Woman Es-el´-lo Baby or Infant

*Transcriber's note: This appears to be a typographical error for "Hot." See "Central Sierra Miwok Dictionary with Texts" by L. S. Freeland and Sylvia M. Broadbent (Publications in Linguistics vol. XXIII, University of California Press, Berkeley, 1960).

NAMES OF THE INDIAN TRIBES PLACED ON THE FRESNO AND KINGS RIVER RESERVATIONS IN 1850 AND 1851.

Names of Tribes— From— Wil-tuk´-um-nees Tuolumne River Yo-sem´-i-tees Yosemite Valley Po-to-en´-sees and Noot´-choos Merced River Chow-chil´-lies Chowchilla Valley Me´-woos Fresno Valley Chook-chan´-cies Fresno and San Joaquin Rivers Ho-na´-ches San Joaquin River Pit-cal´-chees and Tal-an´-chees San Joaquin Valley Cas-was´-sees Fine Gold Gulch Wah-too´-kees, Wat´-chees, No´-to-no´-tose and We-mel´-chees Kings River Cow-il´-lees and Tel-um´-nees Four Creeks Woo´-wells and Tal´-chees Tule Lake